ADDRESS

OF THE

MANAGERS OF THE AMERICAN BIBLE SOCIETY,

TO ITS

AUXILIARIES, MEMBERS, AND FRIENDS,

IN REGARD TO A

GENERAL SUPPLY OF THE UNITED STATES

WITH

THE SACRED SCRIPTURES;

TOGETHER WITH

RESOLUTIONS AS TO THE DETAILS OF THE WORK.

AMERICAN BIBLE SOCIETY'S PRESS.
ASTOR PLACE, NEW YORK.

1856.

TO THE FRIENDS OF THE BIBLE,

OF ALL RELIGIOUS DENOMINATIONS.

GENERAL SUPPLY OF THE UNITED STATES

WITH THE BIBLE.

At the last Anniversary of the American Bible Society, held in New York on the 8th of May, 1856, the following resolution was unanimously adopted by the numerous body of Members present:

In view of the statements made by the Managers in their Report, and with the co-operation of those who view the Bible as indispensable to our civil and religious welfare, this Society now Resolves, *in humble reliance on Divine aid, to enter on a second exploration of our entire country, with the purpose of placing a copy of this Sacred Volume, as early as practicable, in every destitute household where there is a willingness to receive it.*

We give below an address and resolutions, sent forth by the Board of Managers, to aid the Society in carrying out its noble purpose.

ADDRESS.

Dear Friends and Fellow Labourers:—Twenty-seven years ago the American Bible Society adopted a resolution similar to the one given above. On motion of the Rev. Dr. Milnor, seconded by the Rev. Dr. Lyman Beecher, it was,

"Resolved, *That this Society, with humble reliance on Divine aid, will endeavour to supply all the destitute families in the United States with the Holy Scriptures, that may be willing to purchase or receive them, within the space of two years.*"

By the blessing of God, in the course of that time, every accessible family in the more settled portions of our country, was visited, and supplied with the Bible—a noble determination, vigorously executed. At intervals since that period, various localities have in the same manner been explored and supplied; but during the past twenty-five years no systematic and united effort has been made to place this Book within every person's reach, while occasional exertions of our Auxiliary societies in limited fields indicate a general increasing want, and an absolute necessity of the measure now proposed.

In 1829–30 our population was 12,866,000: it is now 26,500,000. Our inhabited territory has increased in equal proportion. Arkansas, Michigan, Florida, Texas, Iowa, Wisconsin, and California,* have been added as States. Territorial governments have been formed in Minnesota, Nebraska, Kansas, New Mexico, Utah, Oregon, and Washington. The necessity for forming such governments shows, that a territory, of more than two million square miles, has been occupied by our increasing population since 1830—a territory twice the size of that country, over which, the charities of the American Bible Society were expanded, in passing the resolution to which we have referred. In the same period the influx of foreigners has increased, from the rate of 23,000, to that of 360,000, in a year; and, although now apparently diminishing, has added to our population, during twenty-six years, more than 3,500,000: a large proportion of these neither bring the Bible with them, nor love its truths. Those who have been willing to receive the Scriptures, have, for several years, been generally supplied, on their landing among us. But the greatest number arrive here prejudiced against the reading of God's Word. A few years' residence within the sphere of our liberal institutions, often proves sufficient, so to relax the bonds of superstition, as to render them accessible to our agencies. When, in addition, we remember the constant invisible operations of the Holy Ghost upon human souls, preparing them to receive with gladness the

* These States were admitted into the Union in that order, and at the following dates; 1836, 37, 45, 45, 46, 48, 50. *Compen. Census, p.* 43.

ingrafted Word, we may well believe, that a majority of this foreign population is now willing to accept, and profit by, a general distribution of the Scriptures.

Ten millions of souls have been born among us within the last twenty-six years. Such a view of the increased field prepares us to estimate certain facts, which have appeared in the experience of our faithful Auxiliaries. We select a few. In the city of Baltimore, and St. Mary's and St. Charles Counties, Maryland, in 1855, after a regular annual distribution, continued through several years, out of 16,000 families visited, 2,200 were found destitute of God's Word. An exploration of the city of New York reveals the fact, that one sixth of the families are without the Scriptures. In the city of Cincinnati, one sixth are destitute; in Louisville, one third. The Virginia Bible Society reports, in 1851, that not less than 8,000 families in that State are destitute of the Bible. In Georgia, of the families visited, a few years since, one third were destitute, and nearly the same at one time in Illinois.

However frequently or carefully distribution may be made, the want increases. Onondaga County, New York, where it might be supposed no serious lack of Scriptures could exist, was visited in 1843; in six years after, one ninth of the families were destitute. Louisville, Kentucky, was thoroughly supplied in 1840; in 1850, one third of the families were destitute. New York city was supplied soon after March, 1849; and although the work had often been done before, 10,800 families were then found destitute.

From such revelations of the dearth of God's Word where our people have received it most freely, you may judge of the destitution among the scattered population, who occupy our Western, and extreme Southern, States and Territories. From New York to Wisconsin, and from Maine to Georgia, including only those States where explorations have lately been made, the ratio of destitution ranges between one third and one ninth. Taking the mean, one sixth, and estimating five in a family, we have the astounding fact, that 883,000 families in our Christian land are utterly without the Bible. Including our Territories, it will probably be much nearer the truth to say, that 1,000,000 families in this country, where God's Word is free to all, never see the Sacred Scriptures.

In presence of such a fact, the American Bible Society feels called upon to address itself again to its great mission. When God discloses such destitution, we must attempt, by his grace, to supply it. No other body of Christian men, in our country, are so well prepared to undertake this act of religious humanity. The American Bible Society therefore approaches the work, with a true sense of its magnitude, but with humble reliance, on Divine aid; and, consequently, with the fullest faith that it will be accomplished. By God's blessing, we intend not to leave one family, in any accessible spot within the United States or its Territories, unvisited, nor, if they will receive it, unsupplied, with the good Word of God.

Our plan goes further. We design to supply all Sunday Schools and youths, with the New Testament at least. They are the hope of the Church. We must lay a good foundation for that hope, by giving them, liberally, the Gospel of Christ. Our plan still further includes the supply of seamen, boatmen, railroad hands, stage drivers, and others in like occupation, with the same blessing. We mean to take advantage of every avenue of commerce, external and internal, to extend a knowledge of the Scriptures. As our ships visit every foreign port, so our boats, our trains, or our stages visit every town and village, and hamlet, of our land. We desire that they shall carry every where a savour of the good Word of Truth. Nor less is it in our minds, that these neglected classes of our community, who, by the necessities of their occupation, are in great measure deprived of other opportunities of grace, shall at least hear God speaking to them messages of salvation from his own Book.

For the accomplishment of such a work we do not limit ourselves as to time; but with our present facilities of communication, we may well hope that our labour will be early completed. Yet if necessary, years must be given to it. "God is never in haste;" and having laid upon us the duty, He will require only that we employ all possible energy.

Our plan depends for its effectiveness, in the first place, upon the zeal and efficiency of our Auxiliaries. When we speak of the American Bible Society, we speak of *them*, as integral parts of its one body. They are its acting limbs. In every district of our country where they are established, the work must be done by them. In those immense districts where it is not possible at present to form branch associations, the Parent Society will endeavour to provide some other instrumentality; but nothing must be expected from it in the way of actual exploration and supply. Where our Auxiliaries exist, exhibiting that life which is in all healthy members of the body of Christ, surely we shall not look in vain for hearty co-operation, and full success.

If our voice can reach any Auxiliaries, which are sleeping on their posts, we beseech them, for the Lord's sake, to awaken to a sense of the responsibility He has laid upon them. For that famine of the Word of God, which is now reducing religion around them to a very spectral life, they are in great measure answerable. While men slept, the enemy has crept in and sown his tares. But an immediate, energetic effort may recover the ground which has been lost. The Lord whom they serve, the Lord who has committed to their stewardship the field in which he cast their lot, expects it of them. Let us count upon the reviving energies, and the now earnest co-operation, of all Bible associations which have suffered themselves to be beguiled into slothfulness.

Our plan contemplates that Pastors and Missionaries, especially those engaged among seamen and boatmen, Sunday School teachers, Bible agents and colporteurs, will associate themselves in this work, or, at least, act in it, in connexion with the local Auxiliaries. Our success depends, not upon rambling effort, however energetic; nor upon spasmodic effort, however enthusiastic; but upon effort in which energy and enthusiasm shall be thoroughly systematized. We therefore urge upon those who are accustomed to lead men, to lend their wisdom to our Auxiliaries, and to take part in some general plan with them. Upon all other Christians, who have, or can make, time and opportunity, for gratuitous service in this great work, we call, with anxious hope that they will devote themselves to it patiently and diligently, until the work is completed. Without doubt, every parish in our country might furnish at least one person, capable of exploring the district immediately within its bounds. Of 38,000 congregations in our land, at least 25,000 are friendly to our effort: probably not less than 20,000 already in some degree co-operate with us. Let us hope, then, but for one labourer in every congregational district, and at once an army of 20,000 agents will be volunteered for this campaign. To organize this force, we ask only that they will severally report themselves to their Pastors as ready for work, and through them act in conjunction with the nearest Auxiliary or Bible agent. These authorities, with whom the Parent Society will communicate, will arrange all details of labour.

The largest portion of the work, we do not doubt, will be accomplished by those faithful women whose hearts the Lord has touched; to whom, like Eunice and Lois, the Scripture of truth has proved hid treasure; and who, in the unselfishness of their nature, cannot but speak freely of what they have found. If we forbear to call upon them for aid, except in general terms, it is only because we *know* that, of themselves, they will be foremost to engage in this labour of love.

Wherever possible we advise that the work shall be done by a voluntary force; for all the funds that can be spared will be needed to enable our presses to meet the increased demand. But where volunteers cannot be found, let paid agents be employed; for by whatever means the intended result must be reached.

Students of theology could scarcely employ vacations more profitably. We invite them to offer their services to the Auxiliary of their district; and we affectionately direct the attention of Auxiliaries to them as likely to prove most efficient helpers, well worthy of confidence and support.

We anticipate effectual assistance from the Christian officers of our Army and Navy—men who so nobly illustrate the grace of God, amidst the difficulties of their profession. They occupy our distant seaports, and those outposts of population, which we shall despair of reaching through any other instrumentality. We direct their attention especially to the destitute border population, to the Indians, and to trains of emigrants and traders in their neighbourhood. We solicit their co-operation in supplying every destitute individual, who can make use of it, with a copy of the Word of God; and we engage to meet liberally all their demands of books for this purpose.

Our plan requires for its completeness, on the part of our Auxiliaries and friends, only one other duty; viz., to provide means whereby the Parent Society may be able to send out copies of God's Word to every quarter. When Auxiliaries order books, let them pay in advance, at least to some extent, if possible. Whenever they have a surplus, let them invest it immediately, and secure an interest for it, in enabling our presses at the Bible House to pour out Bibles for gratuitous distribution. And to friends generally, we say, Let not your hearts grow cold, nor your hands be slack, when we are entering upon the greatest undertaking which has ever engaged the American Bible Society.

Such in brief is our plan. Minor details must be left for the judgment of those, who best understand the several localities. Our watchwords are, System and unity, energy and patience. What we ask is, that every man, woman, and child, whose heart God has touched with the love of Christ, acting either through our Auxiliaries, our Agents, the Parent Society, or some other way, will give themselves heartily to the great purpose of supplying every family, within our extended borders, with the Word of God.

The scheme is large, and therefore worthy of the American Bible Society. Divine Providence proposes small ends to small abilities; but when He raises up a great Institution, gives it a large hold upon the hearts of his people, endows it with great resources, and endues it with a spirit of benevolence, it is that He may accomplish by it great results. We should not act worthily of our position, did we not attempt some great thing for the glory of God, and the welfare of our country.

The enterprising spirit of the age encourages us. Surely force of will within the Church, at least equals that, which, outside of it, accomplishes labours at which the world wonders. The Church always feels the spirit of the age; and when Christianized, it becomes, according to God's appointment, an efficient force suited to her times. Whilst then the children of this world are intensely active, let the enterprise of the children of light be called out and directed. We hold before you the certain promise of gaining souls for Christ; for the Word of God is a life giving seed. It never returns unto Him void; what it touches, it invigorates; where it enters, it enlivens; where it lodges, it germinates, until the whole soul is crowded with evidences of a blessed, spiritual, new life. We propose to you an adventure; not a worldly speculation, but an enterprise in which means are proportioned to the end; which, applied by prayer, and the requisite human labour, must accomplish the end, in which the only venture is that of faith upon the assurances of God. The very spirit of the age encourages us to believe, that Christians will be found prepared to make this venture for Christ's sake. The world engages in great labours, and never wants for means or men. We feel every confidence, then, that this body of Christ and its members will carry their great design to a successful result.

The occasion is opportune. Under God our means are adequate. Contrast our present ability with that which undertook the former general distribution of the Scripture, and you will be convinced that we now advance to no hopeless undertaking. In 1829, the American Bible Society employed only seven travelling Agents, and had only seven hundred Auxiliaries; whereas, in 1856 we number thirty-five Agents, and nearly three thousand Auxiliaries organized in every portion of the field. In 1829 the American Bible Society had been able to accumulate only 360,000 volumes to meet the exigency, and the whole capacity of its presses and bindery was only 300,000 volumes per annum. In 1856 the Society reports the number of volumes prepared for circulation during the past year more than three times this number; with the sheets on hand, in the course of a few weeks, 200,000 volumes could be thrown into circulation; and the capacity of its presses and bindery is not limited even by one and a half million per annum. The Board of Managers feel that God has brought the Society to this eminent position of ability, for the great purpose which his Spirit has now revealed, in actuating them and you, to undertake this proposed thorough exploration and supply of our whole country. His gracious blessing, continually vouchsafed, encourages the effort. The present Annual Report records facts of unequalled interest and animation. By every evidence of the good hand of our God upon us, we are bidden out to new efforts of Christian philanthropy.

Nor are motives wanting. "The love of Christ constraineth us," brethren—that love which has bought us to Himself, and binds us together in one fellowship. The impulses of that charity of God's dear Son cannot but be beating in the souls of all who call themselves by His dear name. Every tie that binds us to Christ Jesus bands us together for accomplishing the mission dearest to His heart. If then there be in you the same mind which was in Him, we know that you will be willing fellow labourers with us in this effort, to spread a knowledge of His great salvation.

We find a motive in the present social and political condition of our country. That selfishness, which equally with enterprise characterizes the times, has loosened social bonds, disintegrated the brotherhood, and taught our countrymen to seek individual welfare rather than the happiness of a united community. The surest corrective of erroneous social ideas, and the truest shield of political stability, are to be found in the principles of the Divine Word. Let us disseminate this charter of our free institutions. Let God's Book teach men not to use their liberty for a cloak of maliciousness, but in love to serve one another; and that then only we are free indeed, when the unselfish, brotherly, loving Spirit of Jesus makes us free. Let us strengthen the position of this corner stone of our political existence, so that it can never be removed from the foundation. In 1777, Congress ordered 20,000 copies of the Bible to be imported for distribution—Congress thus becoming the first American Bible Society. Now that we have been permitted to succeed, to what was then consecrated as a high national duty, inspired by sentiments of holy reverence for Scripture as the very basis of our political institutions, let us place in the hands of every family, within our territory, this charter of our rights and liberty.

We find another motive in the abounding of infidelity. Liberty unchristianized soon degenerates into licentiousness. Perfect freedom of thought, which, when sanctified by heavenly grace, blesses all, becomes a curse when exercised without the sanctions of the Divine Word. Imported infidelity has also largely deteriorated the mind of our country. Much skepticism likewise results from the first unbinding of the eyes of those, who have been educated in superstitious ignorance of Scripture. It indicates the first step of transition from that thraldom and darkness of conscience, into the light and freedom of perfect truth. The process of deterioration, if not hindered, or of transition, if not *rightly* carried out, will be disastrous. The true corrective for infidelity is the free circulation of the Scriptures. We have confidence in God's Word to silence the ignorance of foolish men. The Bible is its own best advocate—its own most effectual vindication; and our country and the times, our Master and his mission, look to us to furnish to every household the Bible; whether as the remedy for the disease, the antidote for the poison, or the preventive for the curse, of infidelity.

Lastly, we find motive in our common desire for the speedy

establishment of our Saviour's kingdom. To that end the distribution of Holy Scripture is an appointed precedent and an effectual instrumentality. Reading the Bible awakens attention to truth. It creates a desire to listen to God's ambassadors. It confirms and sanctions instructions that are according to godliness. It prepares an open door for every other means of spreading a knowledge of salvation, whether by the ministry, by tracts, by Sunday School instruction, or by the visits of colporteurs. All other efforts presuppose this basis—knowledge of and confidence in the simple Word of God: nor can Christ's kingdom ever become universal, until this seed of the Word shall be planted in the intellectual apprehension, and the affectionate belief, of every creature. As then our souls long for the time, when the earth shall be full of the knowledge of the Lord, we must be in earnest in providing every household, and as far as possible every individual, with the truthful words of the living God.

Such is the work, brethren in Christ, in which we desire you to become our fellow helpers—a work whose importance is surpassed by no other effort of Christian benevolence; and whose encouragements and motives combine all that can arouse the energies, or draw out the affections of a Christian soul. It is a work for which we are thoroughly prepared. It is a work which is to employ our hearts and hands unceasingly until accomplished; a work which, in every household of our land, is to lay foundations for the successful ministering of every other means of grace. It is *the* work which all providential circumstances of our position indicate, and all God's blessings poured upon our associated effort demand.

We do not approach such an undertaking with any self reliance. Our help is in the name of the Lord. "I will yet for this be inquired of by the house of Israel, to do it for them," is a Divine direction to us, as to the ancient people. God has, indeed, given us the will; and the work is ours: but the strength is all his own, and the successful accomplishment in his disposal. We call you then, brethren, to prayer, as well as to labour. Let every plan and effort be consecrated by devout supplication. A Divine blessing on our mutual exertions will enable us, to "bring forth the headstone thereof with shoutings of, Grace, grace unto it."

While the details of labour must be left to our Auxiliaries, it is fitting that the suggestion shall come from our Parent Society. That great heart beats healthfully, and all its impulses are quickened by the love of Christ. As its pulsations thrill through every member of the one body, we know that there will be answering motion in every joint and limb. It will be as when a giant wakeneth. We wait trustfully until the American Bible Society, having executed this great benevolent mission, and planted the Word of Truth in every home of our land, under the blessing of God, shall be *felt* to be a power on the earth preparing the way of the Lord.

Signed by order and in behalf of the Board of Managers of the American Bible Society.

THEO. FRELINGHUYSEN, *President.*

THOS. COCK, WM. B. CROSBY,
LUTHER BRADISH, BENJ. L. SWAN,
A. BRUYN HASBROUCK, FRANCIS HALL, } *Vice Presidents.*

J. C. BRIGHAM,
JOSEPH HOLDICH,
JAS. H. M'NEILL, } *Cor. Secretaries.*

HENRY FISHER, *Assistant Treasurer*

CALEB T. ROWE, *General Agent.*

SUBSEQUENT RESOLUTIONS OF THE MANAGERS.

1. *Resolved*, That it be earnestly recommended to the local Bible societies throughout the country to adopt measures for supplying with the Bible, as early as practicable, all destitute families within their respective limits.

2. *Resolved*, That, in prosecuting this work, regard should also be had to children and youth, who have great need of the Scriptures for Sabbath School and other purposes, and who should be furnished with the New Testament, at least, as far as possible.

3. *Resolved*, furthermore, That seamen, boatmen, railroad hands, stage drivers, &c., who are favoured with few Sabbath privileges, have increased necessity for the written Word of God, and should be furnished with it.

4. *Resolved*, That, in entering on the proposed undertaking, it will be for the benefit of all concerned, that a portion, at least, of the funds required for the purchase of books, be raised and forwarded when orders for books are made. The Parent Society will thus be furnished with ready means for preparing books with economy, and the Auxiliaries saved from a protracted, disheartening debt.

5. *Resolved*, That in effecting the proposed supply by the Auxiliaries, it is desirable that the work be performed, as far as possible, by self denying volunteers, each taking an assigned district; and that when hired labourers are necessary, they be sustained, as far as practicable, by the local societies, and aid from the Parent Society, when needed, be sought in the way of books, rather than funds for colportage.

6. *Resolved*, That the various Auxiliaries, as they enter on the proposed supply, be requested to inform this Board when they commence their labours, and also furnish the results when the work is completed, that the same may be published in the Bible Society Record and Annual Reports.

7. *Resolved*, That in portions of the country where Auxiliaries cannot be found, or relied on for supplying the destitute, the Committees on Distribution and on Agencies be instructed to adopt such other methods for securing a supply, as may be deemed most expedient and effective.

What Book for General Supply?

This is a very important question. In too many instances the small type (nonpareil) Bible has been ordered for this purpose, because it is cheap—catalogue or cost price, thirty cents; to Auxiliaries, twenty-five cents. That book, however, is designed mainly for Sunday Schools, and those who have young eyes; but when we come to furnish a book for a *family*, where there are adults, and often aged persons, a larger book should be sought. A distinguished layman in the country, who has devoted much time and attention to the supply of *destitute families*, told our Managers, some years since, that they ought never to furnish a book for *that object* which is worth less than *half a dollar*. This, we believe, is sound advice. The Managers have therefore in readiness for that object a *Brevier Bible*—cost or catalogue price, fifty cents; to Auxiliaries, forty-five cents. This is a book of such size and type that all members of a family can read it. To render it still more valuable, particularly to those who have not a concordance, the headings (or contents) of chapters are reprinted by themselves at the close of the book, so that almost any topic of the Bible is thus easily found.

We give below a specimen of the type of this *Brevier Bible;* and would hope, that while other books are ordered for other purposes, this may be called for extensively to supply destitute families.

11 The Lord gave the word: great *was* the company of those that published *it*.
Psalm LXVIII.

39 ¶ Search the Scriptures; for in them ye think ye have eternal life: and they are they which testify of me.
John V.

11 These were more noble than those in Thessalonica, in that they received the word with all readiness of mind, and searched the Scriptures daily, whether those things were so.
Acts XVII.

15 And that from a child thou hast known the holy Scriptures, which are able to make thee wise unto salvation through faith which is in Christ Jesus.
16 All Scripture *is* given by inspiration of God, and *is* profitable for doctrine, for reproof, for correction, for instruction in righteousness:
17 That the man of God may be perfect, thoroughly furnished unto all good works.
II. Tim. III.

www.ingramcontent.com/pod-product-compliance
Lightning Source LLC
LaVergne TN
LVHW020638110826
845149LV00004B/1270

* 9 7 8 1 4 1 8 1 9 0 4 9 1 *